Playing With

GREVEL LINDOP was born in Liverpool and
he was formerly a Professor of English at th
include *A Literary Guide to the Lake District*; *The Opium-Eater: A Life of
Thomas De Quincey*; and editions of Chatterton, De Quincey and Robert
Graves's *The White Goddess*. He has published five previous volumes of
poems, most recently *Selected Poems* (Carcanet Press, 2000). His website may
be visited at www.grevel.co.uk.

GREVEL LINDOP

Playing With Fire

For Anna
with much love
Grevel
19.iii. 10

CARCANET

First published in Great Britain in 2006 by
Carcanet Press Limited
Alliance House
Cross Street
Manchester M2 7AQ

A CIP catalogue record for this book is available from the British Library
ISBN 1 85754 790 X
978 1 85754 790 0

The publisher acknowledges financial assistance from Arts Council England

Typeset by XL Publishing Services, Tiverton
Printed and bound in England by SRP Ltd, Exeter

For Amanda,
always

Acknowledgements

I owe particular thanks to Chris McCully and Colin Pink, whose encouragement, advice and support during the writing of these poems were invaluable. My gratitude also to the dancers, especially Carina, Lisa and Nicole, for their inspiration and insight. *Beijos!*

I must acknowledge the kindness of Johannes Beilharz, who sent me the German text of the epigraphs from Hoffmansthal, which are taken from his prose poem 'Geschöpfe der Flamme'. The English translations are by Johannes Beilharz and are used with his permission.

Acknowledgements are due to the editors of the following periodicals, in which some of these poems have previously appeared: *Agenda*, *Bonfire*, *The Interpreter's House*, *The Keats-Shelley Journal*, *The London Magazine*, *PN Review*, *Poetry Life*, *Poetry London* and *Temenos Academy Review*.

'Five Lemons' was read as part of the Robert Graves birthday celebrations in Deià, Mallorca, 24 July 2000. 'From the Hexagon, Yndooroopilly, NSW' was broadcast as part of 'Unstill Life: A Sound Portrait of Barbara Blackman's World', produced by Donna McLachlan for ABC Radio, 2002. 'The Snowball' was a prizewinner in the 23rd *Poetry Life* Open Poetry Competition (2003). 'A Dozen Red Roses' won first prize in the 2005 *Poetry London* competition.

'The Peacock' and 'Lighting the First Fire of Autumn' appeared in the anthology *Earth Songs*, ed. Peter Abbs (Green Books, 2002); 'After Baudelaire: "Les Bijoux"' appeared in the anthology *Velvet Heat*, ed. Scott McMorrow (Pretty Things Press, 2005); 'Ekajati' and 'Genius Loci' appeared in the anthology *The Heart as Origami*, ed. Julia Lewis and Padmacandra (Rising Fire Press, 2005); 'Tintagel' appeared in the anthology *Chatter of Choughs*, ed. Lucy Newlyn (Hypatia, 2005).

GL
April 2005

Contents

I

II

III

I

Alle sind Ausgeburten der Flamme. Der Schmetterling: in mir wird die
Intensität des kurzen Lebens und der Gebrechlichkeit zu Farbe...

*We are all creatures of flame. The butterfly: the intensity of a short life and
fragility become colour...*

Hugo von Hoffmansthal

Lighting the First Fire of Autumn

Here they are, the quartered logs in their wicker
basket woven of what I take to be
birch and split willow plaited together,
the copse offering itself for the burning
indoors, twig against twig, tree within tree:

rough-cut block capitals of an alphabet
older than writing: poplar, beech, pine,
chainsawed joints of the wood bled and dried out
for a year, lodged in the season's calendar,
their rituals subordinate, now, to mine

as I build the pyre of oak twigs and newsprint
in the middle of the year's first cold morning.
The TV news shows tropical forests on fire,
drought in east England, and the Midlands flooded,
a crude mosaic of weather that looks like a warning.

St Columcille said he feared death and hell –
but worse, the sound of an axe in a sacred grove.
Now every grove is sacred, and still we burn
wood at times, for the fire also is sacred
and a house without it like a heart without love

when the world heads into darkness. The heat's core
will show you again lost faces and glittering forests,
mountain passes, caverns, an archetypal world
recited in the twinkling of a dark pupil.
The epic buried inside us never rests:

fire is the dark secret of the forest.
The green crowns drink sunlight until their dumb
hearts are glutted with fire. Then, decaying or burning,
give up whatever they have. A match flares
and the paper ignites. Watch, and the poems will come.

Sicilienne

Fauré pours chords across chords and under
my daughter's hands, plunged wrist-deep into the music,
the barred and mottled light of sunshot water
is shadowed into shape, the unexpected
tinge of an arpeggio rippled and glinting
as the tide harps on a rock, and hesitates
then covers it. Repetition is decisive: I'm upstairs
and the music fills the space between the floors
with its lovely tangles, like a chaotic flowering
vine, a mesh of times whose fruit in the heart
is recollected movement. The returning wave
splashing light on the roof of a sea-cave
at Fydlyn plied that tentative pattern as she waded
cautious on pebbles deep-sunk in the cold
summer rockpools, the cave-mouth arching an O
of astonishing turquoise where a seal gazed
back at us, doglike paddling among ribboned
rocks and she climbed out near to it, placing those same
wet hands decisively on the sharp and unwelcoming
stone. Yards overhead seagulls scream and thrift
stars pink on precarious grass, and she is finding
her way back through heavier, less congenial
chords. The weather is changing, August is now
the far mouth to a tunnel of dark seasons
and the stairwell is full of echoes which are the rampaging
of discords on discords back to something simple,
a recurrent time-pattern, something heard but unspoken.
The last chord tolls into distance, endstopped by the
thump of the piano-stool and bang of the door,
decisive step on the stairs, firm evidence
that it's time to go on to something else, something more.

Five Lemons

Here are five lemons from the poet's garden,
the colour of white gold and icy sunshine,
flooded with green around the pointed nipples.
My younger daughter cuts one into quarters,
careful of fingers, bites the white-furred pith out,
devours the quartz-white segments with her eyes shut,
sighing and swaying in the sharp enjoyment.

Here are four lemons from the poet's garden:
one perched on three, a perfect tetrahedron.
The poet's widow showed me where to pick them,
kindly and shrewd, helping me find the best ones,
holding the branch down while I snapped the stalks off,
the cold breeze in our faces from the mountain.
We'll halve this one and squeeze it over couscous.

Here are three lemons from the poet's garden
still in the bowl, turned in a neat triangle,
yellower now. My elder daughter chooses,
after long thought, one for her still-life painting,
the twisted leaves like green airplane-propellers
with a Cezanne pear and a Braque violin,
fractured into art-deco Cubist slices.

Here are two lemons from the poet's garden
below his tall house on the terraced hillside,
red earth black-pitted with his fallen olives
between the gnarled trunks trailing silver foliage,
beside the boulders of the dusty torrent
rainless above that sea of sparkling turquoise.
The juice is perfect for a tuna salad.

Here is a lemon from the poet's garden,
the last of them. Long is the poet gone,
silent his grave on the hilltop under the cypress,
long the shadows drawn by moon and sun
out from the low walls and high gate of the graveyard.
I press the waxy peel to my face and breathe it.
There are no words for what the fragrance tells me.

Mystery

The sun is out again, and the butterflies
elaborate their dance around the garden:
here a white one, there a speckled brown,
sometimes a red admiral or an orange-tip.

Yet for weeks it rained and we didn't see them.
Where do they hide when the globes of rain are hurtling –
shiny projectiles that could punch a hole
clean through their fans of papery silk?

A mystery; like where the word was lurking
until someone asked you for a suggestion –
eleven letters, blank blank PR blank PR –
and without pausing to think, you said 'appropriate'.

At Humphrey Head

Years ago, I looked for a certain spring
on the Cumbrian coast. There were white rocks,
green creepers, bushes, and the lapping sea,
but I could find no spring. I noticed a robin
that perched on a sprig of juniper and sang
a warbling song, flitted a few feet
and sang again. The thought came: *Follow the robin
and you will find the spring.* The bird flew on
from branch to branch and then, suddenly, dropped,
bobbed, sipped. At the foot of the cliff
I found the spring, I drank the medicinal water.

Tintagel

Chough: say it aloud,
letting the breeze carry off
the final consonant.
That way, you hear the cry.

Black as burnt paper
they spiral over the crag,
or strut: scarlet crowfoot
and slant, indigenous eye.

Yes, they have seen it all –
the four Evangelists
staring from golden icons;
oath-taker, shape-shifter,

the king bedding the duke's wife
while the duke goes down in battle.
The fruit will be England's hero.
Now poets and chroniclers

(those carrion birds of legend)
fly up from the hecatomb
crop-full, craw-stuffed –
already digesting the vitals:

out of the strong, sweetness;
out of battle-carnage
the honey of a verse,
gnomic history.

Ash from a thousand books
blows in the quadrangle,
smudging the page as you turn it.
Can you see, on the next leaf –

rubric or marginal gloss,
between the lines, under the black letter –
splayed, windblown, indelible,
scarlet tracks of blood?

Green

Imagine the colours the eye can see as a bow:
the visible spectrum spread out so that violet
is at one tightening end, and deep red the other,
almost ready to touch ends and join in a circle.
At the centre, where an arrow might rest, is green,
the eye's natural target, the centre point
from which the other colours are fanned out:
extrapolated from green into yellow and blue,
but always green is the eye's natural home,
the ruffled green of the oak, the baize of the lawn,
splintered, fractured, sewn, hammered, reflected,
fringe of green at the kerb, rays of green on the walltop.
There's no colour that so much sings of life,
and we are married to it, green is the muscles' bride
as alien and desirable to us as perhaps the red
which is our bloody signature is loved
by the plantworld, which would heal it if it could
and will, with its roots, its kind carbon kisses,
laying our hot words and our anguish asleep
in its mother of leaves, its green gothic windows of light,
its whisper of needles and carpets. The oaktree
is our house and the rowan our protector,
the hawthorn full of advice. Inside the glass,
the brick, the plaster and the concrete, while you read,
every breath you take is the gift of green.

Renaissance

They don't have the repose of the Eastern gods,
the peachlike bloom of the wide-eyed boy Pharaohs,
the floating smile of the Buddha in meditation.
Even the flaming tar-baby Dharma-protectors,
skull-necklaced, holding cups of human blood,
stomping on corpses to clatter their ankle-bells
(deft heel and turned wrist like a Balinese dancer)

are less terrible than these indolent marble giants
whose fleshly perfection, whose blank colossal gaze
speak of a sculptor perfectly obsessed
with self-transcendence. Who, fully believing in God,
took up His creative challenge by carving this
miraculous more-than-humanity out of the stone,
melting the crystal to flesh, tensing the muscle,

sprawling the huge limbs into a massive disdain
for his own antlike, merely human labours.
The new gods are here, at the Fountain of the Four Rivers,
strenuously frozen, their energy poised
on the brink of explosion. What did Bernini intend?
Clearly he would have thought his work well done
if that marble fist had finally uncurled

to wrench chisel and mallet out of his grasp
and fling him onto the heap of marble chippings,
turning to shake its stone siblings awake
and start the revolution. Nearby, at the Trevi
Fountain, the Titans have broken loose from their moorings,
Neptune (but this is not the Roman Neptune)
driving insane white chariot-horses ahead

and almost trampling his own army of tritons
who blow their conches free of the raging water
as the huge shells hurtle forward. 'Get out of the way,
or be crushed by a force already bigger than yours
and constantly gaining momentum,' their gestures say.
Those stone minds already dream of the computer,
the hydrogen bomb, the human genome project,

the assault on the moon. They're not for our contemplation,
but contemplate us. 'Give us time,' they seem to say.
'It will take a few centuries, but what of that?
We will put out God's eyes, pull heaven down on your heads.
A life-sentence means nothing to Titans,
whose lifespan is endless. To think it began with fire!
Enjoy the flames. Prometheus knew what he did.'

Cards from Paris

There's no calendar for the seasons of a life.
Spring may as easily come on the last day
as midway, or at the start of the year.
There's no time but the present, whenever that
may be. So I sit in the Boulevard St Denis,
drinking coffee among the talkers and the shoppers,
while Paris undergoes its oppressive summer;
brought here by a good friend, a love for *The White
Goddess*, a conference on Robert Graves,
resurgence of a buried fondness for France
and other things too nebulous to mention.
Today I visited the rue de l'Échiquier,
but the Mayol, my adolescent temple, was gone,
the rhinestone-spangled G-strings of the dancers
and the blue ostrich-feathers untraceable,
indelible in memory like wall-paintings
in a pyramid, nude dancers flowing to music,
still watched by someone who is no longer there.
And somewhere on the Butte de Montmartre
under the mushroom-cluster of Sacré Coeur
must be the shop where the old lady sold me,
kind and smiling, that pack of novelty cards:
an incarnation of Madame Sosostris,
dealing me the hand – cards on the table –
which would govern my life. The naked strawberry blonde,
the redhead with small breasts, the brunette
with suspenders and black stockings. Then they were dreams
but I would meet them all later, make love to some,
merely desire others, get bored with a few, marry
the one most beautiful to look at and most
delectable to touch. But so little would change
inside. I am still fourteen and a half,
my exact age the night I sat in the Mayol.
And probably always will be, though they bulldoze
the theatre to build a Monoprix,
though Paris is mostly towerblocks and flyovers.
There are patterns in us like watermarks in paper,
and some don't change. Despite the heavy traffic,
my fellow tourists and the pneumatic drill,
I shall order another coffee and see it through.

The Cypress Trees

Waking at night, in darkness, I stepped out of bed,
knowing perfectly well where I was:
bare wall at an angle, door at the end,
tall shuttered window. And outside
the long garden with the cypress trees –
the moon-shadows, the gentle Italian night.

All wholly familiar; only my hand
struck a wall where no wall should have been.
I felt along it. The door was missing too.
Perplexed, not frightened, I still knew the place –
polished wood floor of the passage outside,
white plaster wall. Yet the door wasn't there,

the wall was in the wrong place. Then I remembered:
I was at home, in England, no longer in Rome,
where I'd slept last night. But far stranger than that,
though I touched my English wall, this room my mind
insisted I stood in was not in the Roman hotel –
the mirrors, the yellowy light from the via Margutta –

not at all. This was some unknown Italian room,
yet intimately familiar. I was lost –
laughed, almost, at the metaphysical comedy
of touching a room I was quite unable to picture
whilst mentally standing in one at a different angle,
in another country, unidentified

yet thoroughly known. At last, groping my way
to the actual door, I grasped a knob. And then
my room came clear in my head, as if a light
were suddenly switched on. Where had I been? –
awake, alert, amused, and somewhere else.

I'm patient enough. Perhaps I shall get back there.
Will it be with fear? Glad recognition?
Elusive, troubling sense of *déja vu*?
Enough that I remembered; or that the place,
for its own peculiar reasons, remembered me –
the slant wall, the high, shuttered window,
the unseen blue moonlight. The cypress trees.

Hen Felin

There is a white house sunk in the long grass
and a spring rises, no one knows from where

and there is nothing, nothing and again nothing.
The nothings talk together in the house.

The beach breathes when the tide hisses along it,
each pebble bald as a moon; and the moon rises,

and the rocks melt and wrinkle the bright sea.
Part of me has been living here for years

among the nothings and the silences
which are not nothing and are never silent.

And stranded under the long grass and the weeds
a wooden boat, her timbers sprung by time

the white wood mildewed, SWALLOW on the bow:
a white moon drowning in a green sea.

The knitwork tapestry of furballed goosegrass,
pink spikes of willowherb have run her through

but still the unstaunched spring whispers and sings
and will not let her rest and turn to earth

but long past hope still sets the empty heart
echoing to the perpetual music of water.

How Long Is the Coast of Britain?

It could be a year ago
and I am treading on stones
weedcapped and bedded in sand,
water oozing between my toes
as I look up to trace
my children running, shouting
but shrunk almost to points
on the shining flats, drawing a line
in front of the restless cold blaze
of a far-out tide. Nothing has changed;
at that distance they seem no larger
and though they are still running
no distance seems covered. As the gull flies
we're not so far from New Brighton
where I did the same thing at the same age,
if I had an age. The memory
carries no mark of time, cannot be placed. I remember
slippery rocks, the girders of the pier
shaggy with an ogreish velvet
of emerald weed, and dragging a spade on its edge
as I ran, to draw a minuscule furrow miles long,
as it seemed, as it seems. The scale must be wrong. How far
is it now? You could walk
from here to there, I suppose, taking in bays
and headlands, Caernarvon, the Great Orme, the Wirral,
the distance lengthening
far beyond the road's approximate windings
as you paced the furrows of sand, the stone quays,
barnacle-blistered rocks and the crackling stringy
wreckage of the tide-line, lost shoes and plastic bottles.
And that would tell you nothing
of the true distance. Follow a sand-hopper
or a small spider, those arcs and anxious scuttlings
deviating round boulder and sand-heap, mountaineering
over pebble after pebble, zigzagging
round the root-fingers of the marram-grass:
the line becomes an endless filigree,
yet still cutting corners, for the pebble
is a fissured pavement of disjunct crystals, the sandgrain
a fishnet labyrinth of molecular silicates. Every measure

23

has other measures inside it, and inside those. The ragged
path from here to childhood might be like that:
a contour traced by simplification across
crevasses, a spider's thread thrown over
the honeycombed surface
of memory, each cell
an involute of other cells, moments
and perceptions within moments, and memories
within perceptions. Here
the cliffs are stratified
like layers of paper-ash, a hecatomb
of burnt books; and there are fossils
in the carboniferous pages, though I can't find them.
Better the Dorset cliffs, where the rain brought down
curlicue ammonites cast in fools' gold,
spiral nuggets to be kept in a box
and fingered, the metal helix
of the shell a trace of that lifetime's growth
like the unicorn shells and pink-fluked convex fans
picked up yesterday on the hard
brown ribs of sand to be prized and forgotten,
crushed on the carpet, found in a pocket
or a dream years later. Time
is a line as elusive as the fractal curve
of any coastline – the seasons since we were here
have lifetimes in them,
churned mud and snow on the lawn,
my son flying a Chinese
bird-kite of brilliant paper in the humming wind
at Formby, where the oilslick
has fouled the dunes now; or the quarry in Wales
where my daughter found her first fossil,
a minute fan-shell
etched pristine on a gunmetal flake of shale,
and stood there yelling, three years
with twenty million in her hand. I can feel the sun
still on the blinding dust of the quarry-tip,
and the dust on the fingerprint ridges
of my fingers. Nothing gets lost or ends. Yesterday
he carried a small jellyfish to the sea
in his bucket: it was beautiful,
he said; he wanted to save it
from stranding on the beach. Wrong-side up

at first, it righted itself, a pulsating
crystal saucer, and huffed itself away
into the tide. Now he's hunting crabs
as he did just here a year ago, winding
his way towards me down the gleaming
bars where the shallows flood irregularly
with the incoming water. I can't get back
to the last time I walked here, let alone
to being his age. The more I can recall
the more there is to be recalled, how I got here
from that small boy is inconceivable, the curve
of time folds in and complicates
when you would look at it. I walk to meet him
along the current of a stream
that runs continually, fresh water into salt,
meeting the tide, setting up a balance
whose limits can't be found or mapped.
A crest spills over
shrinking the sand behind the girls. A lifted stone
reveals an olive shield that vacillates
then pounces for the centre of the pool. He scoops it out
and holds it up, delighted. Here and now
everything's clear; but it's the boundaries
that give us room to live. Nothing's emptied,
however long we look. 'Coastline length
turns out to be an elusive notion', we're told;
attempts at measurement tending to show
the typical coastline's length as 'very large
and so ill-determined
that it is best considered infinite'.
And as for what we are, calculating that's
a journey like travelling in and in
among the seahorse tails and spumebursts
of the Mandelbrot set, or watching the lace and eddy
of the tide lipping the rocks, washing and interpreting them again,
lost and renewed like memory, elaborating a line
infinite and bounded like the life of a man.

Taking Down Cavafy

Taking down Cavafy today, I recognised
how books from that era have a certain look –
from that era of my life, I mean:
from perhaps 1966 to '77.
There's something fermented about them, a kind of patina:
browned like autumn bracken by natural
process of acidity, damp
and foxing like rainspots on the paper,
they are also often thick
with a furry dust along the tops, dust which survived
the subsequent moves, a mulch compounded
of ash from the incense I ceaselessly burned,
from the housedust of tawdry, wornout bedsits
and student flats, and perhaps from the cigarettes
I haven't touched now for nearly thirty years
as well as the bedroom (often there *was* no bedroom) motes
from the blankets, the moulting pillows,
the dying mattresses where I made love
with a series of girls as remote and unbelievable
now as Pompeian frescoes. And there's something else
on the pages. What is there when I open the book
is not the poems I recall but other readings,
poems another person laid on the surface
of the words, expectations and ideas
incomprehensible now. They were spread there
often at 3 a.m. or on dull afternoons,
to a soundtrack of Mahler or the Grateful Dead,
when nothing (and more importantly, nobody)
was happening. They are made of unfulfilled
desires – which Cavafy says look like
the beautiful dead, shut in their mausoleum
'with roses at the head and jasmine at the feet'.
But they are the desires of someone else
who has left the books to me. I'm glad to have them –
the books, that is – and read the poems now
trying to clear, yet guiltily tasting, the old readings that persist,
as I wiped – half reluctantly – the dust from the head of this book,
and savour the encroaching brown, the foxing,
the acidity nothing will take away.

II

… the fire and the rose are one.

T.S. Eliot

To Circe

Others have come to grief
tempting the snout or gill
or shagged, wrinkled hide:
gulping a pure desire
provoked to envious rage
whatever partial beast
ungainly hulked inside.

Nor do I fail to take
the cup you reach, to drink
and drinking meet your eyes;
nor are the creatures dead
your wine would summon out
to whelm the human host
and tear him where he lies.

I am them all and more –
crazed wolf and generous lion,
eagle, self-pleasing dove
and dumb, omniscient fish
lend to this changing heart
the force with which they live:

no sudden beast can tug
its hood over this skin
where all are known for such.
Your baffled magic runs
to earth. Believe your eyes,
this is the human face
your eager fingers touch.

The Snowball

Hard to believe, I know, but her name was Bonnetête,
Catherine Bonnetête; and, yes, she gave it.
Just seventeen, fresh out of school, she had
a storm of dark hair with sparks in it, and eyes
so deep you saw yourself in them and still
wondered what she was thinking. Mostly I thought
only about how slim she was, and how
her breasts were small, but full enough to sway
like bells above me when she leaned forward
to do what she did best. I could be patient –
a gift in the dark knife-edged days of a winter
near Zürich, as the white steam flowered
from pipes in the farmhouse roofs and the candied frost
gave way to tantrums of snow that rattled the windows.
Taking a long time was a virtue then,
and I hoped when she leaned deeper into her job
for the gentle avalanche of that long dark curtain
across my skin before she would sit back
to drag the whole mass over her head, one-handed,
and fix it, stretching the hairband in her teeth,
before bending back to her task. But when she achieved
that slow-coming winter flower she had nurtured
so long, and the whole thing exploded and stilled,
I was surprised, that first time, as she rolled
over, pulled my face towards hers, and tongued
me a long strange kiss, a kiss from a liquid planet.
No one had done it like that. Who was she, and what
did she offer my mouth? Something that has stayed,
some oracle, some knowledge of what she knew
about me, something that burned perhaps in her throat
and had to be uttered. One of the many muses,
it seems, though we parted thirty years ago,
and the scene has turned to one of those glass bubbles
with a farm and a yard and a forest inside, and two
little figures. Tilt it a bit and the blizzard starts,
and you wonder what it all means, what you have lost,
until the drifts settle down and you go still
and shelve it. Where are we now? And where is the wood
the farmer was burning the day I left? As I drove
out of the yard, I could see in the rearview mirror

just what I see now: the sheds, the farmhouse, a light
in an upstairs window, a chainsaw abandoned on snow,
and the piled brushwood burning up as the blizzard closed in,
its white clouds tinged with the tongues of fire.

Maison de Jouir

Gauguin: Musée d'Orsay

Soyez mysterieuses
Soyez amoureuses
Et vous serez heureuses

Edging the dark door,
how the mahogany words implore
from depths you had not seen before

shadow-rouged, dreaming girl,
sea-god eyed and navel'd mother-of-pearl,
lost heart tugged and looped in the sea-wave's curl

sweeter than morphine
uncharted ocean of the girl's skin,
tainted, oracular currents of the blood within

from shuttered blue of night
red clay and bougainvillea burnt with light,
winebottle cooled in deep well far from sight.

Brown skin and raven hair,
smooth shoulders kissed and fondled everywhere
and *Yes*, she says, *in French the word is jouir.*

Shattered billows come
shivering the beach. A dark door whispers *Come.*
Tu jouis? Gently she insists. *Yes, now you come.*

Only the surf that whispers
only a girl's small fingers
only the lost heart that remembers:

Soyez mysterieuses
Soyez amoureuses
Et vous serez heureuses.

Perfume

'It was a perfume for a dark-haired girl,'
you said, pressing your wrist against your cheek
for what seemed a long time. 'It had a trace
of something like patchouli, and vanilla…'
(You'd breathed it fully so you must have known.)
There was no dark-haired girl, at any rate
not in your thoughts, only the words you spoke
later, explaining why you hadn't bought
that one for our blonde daughter. But I noticed
the opening beauty of your phrase, the way
like an unstoppered flask it filled the air
with hints, nuances, visions, the whole drift
of what I love in you, my dark-haired girl.

Myth

So many things to make a galaxy:
the flutter of my tongue between your lips –
butterfly shivering a salted rockpool,
breaking the sea's meniscus into tumult;
your hands, moulding me up like growing clay;
your mouth, tasting and ripening what you'd made;
you, turning over, pulling me on top;
the elements combining, heavens opening,
primeval floods.
                        Then how you sighed and stretched,
shook a night sky of hair back from your face
and, with the lazy splendour of a goddess,
strolled to the bathroom; leaving in your wake
that trail of white stars on the bedroom floor.

Nights When You Wake

Nights when you wake and worry about our daughter
(living on casual work in Lanzarote)
I let your words run into the velvet dark,
a silence I hope is comforting. It is
the curves and contours of a mountain landscape
I trace across your back, over your breasts,
raising a gentle harvest of awoken
down that blooms your skin somewhere between
peach and nettle – the openness of love,
the prickly troubles of an anxious mother
that can't be sated now or ever settled.
Day will lighten it all, there isn't much
right now a moneygram can't mend for her,
and though it costs, it will all settle down.
I stroke your back like moulding clay or music
out of the darkness. Then I run my tongue
between your shoulderblades. You gasp and wriggle
and happier now you roll across towards me,
we bathe ourselves a little in the love
our daughter came from, like a healing pool
that's poised somewhere among volcanic mountains,
a cool refreshment in abrasive basalt,
and float to sleep, focusing on some knowledge
deeper than words or touch, deeper than dreams.

Pearls

Tonight you wear pearls, the living gems of the sea,
and these are from Taiwan, spoil of an island
gemmed itself in the troubled ripples of ocean,
a grain in the planet's pearl. There at the heart
of each is the grit, the nacre clouding around it
as fantasy clouds and lustres the pain of desire,
the grit in the heart – the rosary bead of love
sphered round an ache of wanting. Pearls must be fed,
must be worn next the skin so they breathe and bathe in the body's
aura, its sweat, its sweet hormonal tropics
as these do now, a string of little moons
singing to that other sea inside you,
to the sandalwood of your breasts, the forests of hair
that shake and tumble each time your shoulders bow,
as your breasts sway and you tower like a goddess of rose
quartz, of ivory, a living icon over me
while the pearls glisten and click, their gentle current
awake in each separate orb to the tides of rhythm
and the music of our touch, your opening breath
invoking, invoking the subtle elusive moment,
the sheer drop, involuntary prayer, your hands
at work as if pressing clothes, your concentration
bright as the pearls, settling and hardening, its focus
of expectation sharpening as you bring us
to the point, force me to fill you with my pearls.

Closure

For Barbara Herrnstein Smith

She might have been Malay or Vietnamese,
anyway slim, longhaired and unbelievably
willing. After long searching each other's mouths
(neither of us having said a word to try
if we shared a language or just a confusion of tongues)
my mouth found itself against other lips,
her hips circling and pressing, until it seemed
to be almost time.
               Then suddenly I was
inside her (though from another point of view
all this was, of course, inside me) and
as it approached, I was tasting her breasts.
Sadly it was too good not to wake from:
it wasn't I who melted first, but she.
I never found out how it was supposed to end.

Glossolalia

I thought I'd heard it all,
but this time didn't know what was happening.
Inside/out of what language were you speaking/singing?
Where did it come from? Were you
a Minoan priestess, a Pythoness
from Delphi with forked tongue
and lexicon of riddles,
or a Voodoo *houngan* ventriloquising
Erzulie or Maman Brigitte?
Your utterance
ran on with the fluency of bubbles
that stream from a loop held by the hand of a child
to the wind, or the ribbon of notes I'd heard unfurling
from the guitars of Carlos Santana and John McLaughlin;
more intricate than the ululations of Grace Slick on *Bark*.
I thought I knew the gamut
already: the little sighs
and murmurs; the tentative *mm?*;
the gasps; the moans of those girls
who tried to emulate the too-shrill squeals
of the videos (*omigod! omigod! harder! harder!*)
But this was something else, you were translated
somewhere different, and as we fell into rhythm
you sang and recited rhapsodies in an
unknown, unknowable language, musical
and fluent, surprising and ecstatic,
tuning my own delight higher and higher
with the sheer amazement of it, the intuition
of something secret opening around us
as you approached the point of no return
speaking with more than tongues, touched by a fire
that flowered at your mouth
unforgettable, those few times, that blessed us both.

A Dozen Red Roses

This one's for the wine: all those burgundies,
Merlots, Cabernet Sauvignons, the Shiraz,
Blossom Hill, Gallo, Chilean
and so on and on; each bloodrich with the taste
of what happened and what might have happened. Next
one for the kiss, first kiss and last and those between –
they're all nested together like layers of crystal, the
intense and the perfunctory, the brush
of the lips and the biting, the sucked, the tongued-in,
the ones that shake in the seizure of orgasm,
the goodnight, the goodbye, the burrowing into your neck,
I could go on but they're all one, petals of a single
rose that keeps flowering. And this third rose is the heart,
dilating and contracting as you open
the door or the letter, pick up the phone, listen
or are disappointed. (For 'you' also read 'I'.)
Frivolous fourth is for the lipstick: Cool Cinnamon,
Ruby Kiss, Fireball and the rest, an evening's
stage lighting applied with a painter's art
then wrecked with abandon or squandered on hands, tissues,
glasses, cheeks, the unnoticed margins
of where you went and what you did; and twinned
fifth and sixth, these for your nipples, firming to buds
one by one between my lips, raspberry
or coral, round them the delicate
frosted peach of your breasts, the skin awakened
to a *frisson* by my touch, a shudder of cool air
or, in sleep, by the spiderweb fringe of nightmare
trailed across your dreamflesh until I comfort you,
fitting body to body and murmuring, murmuring.
Seventh, a magic number for all my fantasies,
the times when we slept apart, my invocation
of you on top of me, under me, opening to me:
your mouth, your knees, your unexpected fingers
conjuring even in imagination
more out of me than I knew I had:
turning the other half-dreamed women formless,
fading them to transparencies, to less than ghosts,
with the full fury of your imagined presence
lit by desire, more tangible than longing,

an absence solider, more penetrable
than the being of anyone else. And eighth are the perfumes
you liked most, Diorella, Diorissimo,
Tendre Poison, Opium, anything
deep and musky and smelling of roses,
planting memories deep inside the body,
incarnating your presence, your absence, a breath in, a breath out.
Ninth, the Muses' number, are the poems
I wrote you; and those I read by your light –
a glow that flared them from within
like paper lanterns with a fire at the heart:
poems of Yeats, of Graves, of Sir Thomas Wyatt,
of Neruda and Baudelaire, poems fragrant
with the subtle, starry sweat of the shivering mind
and the constellations of wind that chime their answers
to our breath, as the last stars answer the dew
on the leaves, moved by the same forces. And the tenth rose
is time, not a line but a perpetual
unfolding, out of nothing richly into
nothing, the eye – where we live – of an unrelenting
slow hurricane, millefiore of moments
reflecting each other, rose window of instants,
layered and nourishing with the exchanges of love.
The eleventh is for your own, your secret rose,
the bud and the petals, answering to my touch
or your own, delicate and dewed, intent focus
of the body's adventurous projections, compass-rose
of its more-than-spatial map; eclipser of pride.
And the twelfth is a rose. Just a rose.
And is there a thirteenth, O an ominous extra?
Indeed there is, though unseen here, an offering
to the furies, to the kindly gods
that all our secrets stay secret, that the roses fade
and fall only with the end of our own day
which will be just the one, however far
apart its dawn and night, the hours between
falling in like petal on petal, each one deeper
and richer than before, all the way down
until the last, the invisible rose is content.

That Month

That time it took more than a week,
the ruby gently seeping and persisting
each time you checked. The stain
was still there after ten days
as if the wine drew near its lees,
the biological clock were running down.

We made love with the usual passion
and playfulness, though now
perhaps it was an autumn
in here as well as outside. Time of ripeness,
our love sweet and lined
as the apples I picked all too soon

from the young tree
under the brown lilacs.
We told each other truthfully
each of us looked younger than ever
and more beautiful,
and it all felt better than ever, my potency

a fine art without function,
all practical purpose removed
with those two half-inches of translucent tube
like sections of empty red biro refill
the surgeon showed me before
closing the titanium clips

and stitching me up, leaving sex
a matter of rhetoric
and delight, useless and meaningful as poetry.
We wondered, though, how many more such months
there would be.
Not that it mattered greatly in itself –

The chain already linked, our granddaughter
well on the way, a curled shadow-puppet
blooming
in the scan's lunar haze of black and white,
our reproductive days a mirage,
slipping

towards the edge of Nature,
only memory's DNA
still twirling its involutes, labyrinths of love and beauty
unfolded to a frail staircase aspiring toward some music
that might transcend
our sweet murderous biological mother.

The Mirror

I can even date it,
with the meaningless
jingle of numbers,
the necklace we make to hang
(as children might a daisy-chain)
round the lovely neck
of the infinite and eternal.
It was January the thirteenth,
nineteen seventy-seven,
and I was consumed in the embrace
of a nymph of pure flame.
Someone might speak of tongues, hands,
eyes, shoulders and lips,
but for me there was only the consuming
and consumed, the raging
of a desire at once
insatiable and satisfied.
And now when I remember,
these are hot tears that come to my eyes
and they are the tears of joy
for what is neither lost
nor permanent. Already I see
that when King Yama's court
opens its doors to me,
and I have bowed before him
full of that last happiness
of being free, if only
for a little, from the jaws of time,
he will hold up his mirror
and what will shine within it
will be a scarlet rowan tree
and I a green vine around it,
will be a white waterfall
and I a salmon who leaps it,
will be the moon and the sun
locked in their mutual eclipse;
and the fire of their interlocking
is what burns me now, love, and you.

To Ekazati

A Tibetan protecting deity

Lady with one plait, one eye, one tooth,
dancing implacable on the glittering palace
of bones which is this world where we shall all
die, and most have died already, love
of my life, I offer you this skullful of blood
which is a poem spilled out on the page.
Suck out the marrow from my bones, drum
on my distended skin, unpick my sinews
and tune them for your lute-strings. All of me
is gone already but that ball of fire,
my heart, lost in the burning sea that time
and passion fling around us like napalm
or permafrost. Lover, mother, protector,
guiding me in the maze of seven circles,
embrace me. I shall know you in the dark.

III

¿Por qué te vas tan lejos
de la plazuela?

¡Voy en busca de magos
y de princesas!

*Why do you go so far
from the little square?*

*I go in search of magicians
and princesses!*

Federico García Lorca

Ars Poetica

Whoever dreams the schedule up has certainly
got it right today: Carina and Nicole
both working this lunchtime, and here I am with the whole
afternoon to spend. Blowing away behind me
Clerkenwell vanishes as I swing the door into the bar,
the warm dim light, the smoke-flavour, and there they are,
Nicole just coming offstage settling a red dress
and Carina in a white basque, relaxing in the darkness
of a corner table. Welcome to the cavern of making,
the dreamworks, where the man behind the bar checking
the optics adjusts adjectives and the mirrors set free
cascades of oblique images out of memory,
and the girl who's next to go up on stage in her blue
PVC skirt and halter top is a spontaneous, true
(yes) metaphor for rhythm, or a simile
for the decorative application and discarding of words. Meanwhile we
kiss and swap news. What now? Drinks, obviously:
for Carina white wine (it has to be Jacob's Creek);
cranberry juice (no ice) for Nicole; and a Becks for me. They speak
in a purr of Portuguese, another fragrant strand in the music,
while I wait in the spectrum of Aftershocks and Bacardi
Breezers, the sweet savours of coloured glass already
melting (trapped souls singing in bottles), then turn away,
balancing three glasses, three meanings, so they poise
in delicate triangulation.
                              I'm spoilt for choice.
Who shall I ask first, the dark muse or the blonde,
the sunflower's gold petals or the dark centre plunging beyond
what can be guessed or spoken? Do I want Comfort or Despair
to plant her polycarbonate heel on my shoulder, throw her hair
over me in a burst of light or a black tropical storm?
But not so fast. Don't hurry. The poem needs a form,
a pace, a structure. We have to start slow,
and we talk about what we're reading. Nicole wants to show
us the Avon catalogue (we help her choose between Frosty
Apricot and Uptown Pink) and the *Daily Star* horoscopes have to be
dissected. I'm taking a course in astrology
so we check out Gemini, Libra and Cancer but can't
quite decide if Justin Toper is better than Russell Grant.
I've brought Elizabeth Bishop's *Anthology*

of Twentieth-Century Brazilian Poetry.
Who does Carina like? Carlos Drummond de Andrade,
though I argue for Cecília Mereiles
and 'Segundo Motivo da Rosa': I tell Carina she's
the *bela e interminável rosa*, eternal rose
transmuting itself into time and perfume and verse
right now as we sit here. It all goes into the mirrors,
the colours are classic and kitsch and the huge DJ
is loaded with gold chains, every CD
flashes a rainbow at us startling and momentary
as the eye-contact of the girl on stage
when she bends forward to offer us her cleavage
or the vertical splay of reflections in the chrome pole
she winds herself round like a flame, moving and still
reflected.
　　　　　　But the drinks are finished, it's time for art or business.
Who'll give me a dance first? This time Carina will,
so we head for the curtains and as we go I can feel
the delight and the sadness ignite, and start to distil,
again, the ordinary alchemy. For here nothing is real
and everything is possible, this is the Green Cabaret,
Blue Angel, Moulin Rouge, Cabinet of Dr Caligari
and we are all on stage, we are all lost
in our own and each other's imaginations. The drinks cost
only pub prices, entrance is free
and nothing is hidden or true or lied about. Believe me,
all that goes on in here is pure poetry.

Table Dance

Forget the table, there isn't one. Nicole
likes American rock music, and un-
dresses in red, just the bra top,
wisp of lace for a skirt, and the G-string –
though the perspex stilettos might hint
at some fairy-tale beginning, glass slippers
of a Cinderella who stayed out far too long
after midnight and never went home.
Now she twirls on glittering toes, grasps
the pole as if to turn the world upside down
but it's herself she spins, and I'm amazed
at how high over me she can kick,
at how low she can bend and still look back
between her legs at me, that enigma,
those eyes unreadable. But when she comes close –
the podium dripping with discarded red –
it isn't those dark curves or the almost-splitting
fruit of her labia, nor even the poppy
burn of her mouth that I must watch. And no,
I won't always follow her hand down
to that teased nipple, or the gossamer preen of her
finger tracing sweet involutions of self-
love between her thighs. No, it's the eyes I go for:
beyond their diamond-burst that far darkness
where nothing's faked or has a price, where we
are both naked, and we know what we know.

The Net

Carina's netted like a lovely fish
   or mermaid who's been caught up in a trawl
of tiny jetblack beads. Over the rose flesh

     the crisscross texture clings, glistening like oil.
Look, she says, *this is something I wear*
   when I feel happy. She wants to show me all

she knows about dancing, so I go with her,
   drawn by her blue eyes, Latina laughter, the gleam
of rippling reticulation, and that blonde hair

     all over her shoulders. It's a topologist's dream
the way she slides the black bra off and never
   disturbs the dress, whose sticky co-ordinates seem

to map her breasts more intimately than ever,
   a lover's fantasy how her nipples make
it through the gaps. She squeezes her breasts either

     side of the pole, scrunching them up to take
beads clashing against metal (Baudelaire
   you would have loved it) then with that sinuous, snake-

like wriggle, loses the knickers too. And there
   she is, completely clothed, completely naked,
the waveform of her body seducing the square

     mesh to a shimmer. Non-Euclidean,
all co-ordinates fall together as she
   lets the dress drop to a black bitumen

pool on the carpet and I suddenly
   understand how I'm inside the net,
it's woven of looks and gestures so intimately

     twisted there's no possible way out. Yet
just like a shining spider's web, that thread
   is sticky with vestiges of love. Forget

whatever you heard, whatever you expected,
  what you have to hide. Here there is only
a woman's body and a man's naked

  looking; and now she reaches to show me
that secret which, however often revealed,
  will always stay a secret. Carina, let me

wrap you in words, think somehow you're furled
  subtly under these lines, that like a star
whose light takes aeons to reach us you're recalled,

  glimpsed, dancing, when this is read, however far
off, years away, lifetimes distant, now the song's over –
  though such things, as we both know, never are.

Afterwards

Afterwards mostly we talk, on one of the Baroque
sofas in the curtained area, poised on the bright dazed spell
cast by the lenses of the tiny tilted
surveillance cameras up in the corners.

Voyeurs of voyeurs, they will ensure
our images are floating
blue and lined, voiceless and spectral
on the screens in the office, supposing anyone cares.

What do we talk about? Sex, mostly.
Also about work, about poetry,
about who's travelling where
and about how we feel about what we're doing,

whatever that is. What *are* we doing? Is it
damage or therapy, something that might save
a life or wreck it? I have no idea.
I don't think you have either.

Did I use poetry like a tin-opener
to enter your life? Some might say so.
I think you would have told it all to me anyway,
but now we'll never know. The poetry is there,

just as the cameras are, noticing the empty poles and podia,
or the people who arrive in twos and threes,
some to take all their clothes off while they talk
and laugh, then dress and go away again.

There's a peculiar comfort
in knowing that our fantasies, obsessions,
our sheer and unadulterated strangeness
are what drove us here: two aliens

from separate galaxies, conversing weirdly in the airlock
of a far-flung space station: saved and wrecked,
bizarre beyond belief, hugely elated
by the utter difference which is what we share.

Brazilian

What was that film? *Wild Orchid*, with Carrie Otis.
Well, I never liked orchids. But the colours were right –
bougainvillea purple, and the torrents
of some scarlet blossom like what I recall of your lips,
the sudden kiss of them like the wingbrush
of a huge butterfly. Brittle. Silksoft.
Your nipples when you offered them were black like charcoal,
your breasts sheened darker than mahogany or teak
but soft as living shadow and as impalpable.
I'm just one of your lost travellers, doomed
never to come back, never to make it,
poisoned with unbearable sweetness and mythical
riches, my eyes fixed to the last breath
on a glimpse of the tropical forest refined
to its essence, a lush and delicate tract leading
towards a perfumed and unattainable valley.

Watching

Watching as she took off all her clothes,
he unwrapped his own heart's desire
only to find another desire inside it,
another and another.
Inside each desire a new pleasure,
a new pleasure with a new sorrow in it,
a new inside with a new outside around it,
a new she, unwrapping a new him.

The New Girl

She wears white platform boots and a pink corset,
knickers to match. She gets the other girls,
the more experienced ones, to check her over,
straighten her costume. They laugh around the table.
Most of them are speaking Portuguese.
She was scared beforehand, but it was easier
than she expected. Much easier. Now
she's done it for two weeks and she's adept
already. As soon as she's on stage
(if you can call this tiny carpeted surface
a stage) she's caught the eye of a huge man
in front of the bar, and dances as if just for him
(which I admit makes me slightly jealous),
undulating against the pole's silver,
the pink ribbons snaking over her shoulders,
tossing her long hair back, flashing her eyes.
She has dark skin and European features,
a perfect Brazilian beauty. You'll either like
the two tattoos, one on each shoulder, or you won't.
Her body is perfect too: slender, lithe, with lovely
(not large) breasts, one with a silver ring
through the nipple. A student of journalism,
she keeps a diary of all this and one day
will write a book about it. But just now
she takes the knickers off, caresses herself,
explains to each of us how well she knows
how much we'd like to give her those caresses.
And we like to know this, like to be known,
to know ourselves and know she does this knowing.
Her body is the mirror of that knowledge,
much deeper than the skin, and quite unmarked:
clear as a pool, untouched, still, the new girl.

Shoes

'With naked foot stalking in my chamber' –
The words float up as I watch two of the girls
prowling the bar, trawling for private dances.
Believe me, Sir Tom, they stalk even better
in five-inch stilettos; though truly none of these
has done it in my chamber, nor ever likely to.
Alexandra kicks hers off before she goes on stage
and lets the DJ mind them. So fast she dances,
spinning around the pole, flipping herself
upside down and then sliding to earth
gripping by just one leg, shoes would impede her,
but she's the only dancer I've seen
naked all the way up to the footsoles.
The others sport the usual perspex heels,
black strappy uppers or slingbacks, and Nicole favours
thighboots, today the grey suede ones, the longest
boots on the longest legs I ever saw.
And I recall how Amanda kept her shoes on
when I asked, and clasped me tighter so I could feel
the heels in my back as we made love. What was the magic?
I don't know; but the clothed is what allows the naked,
as death allows life, as the present allows the past
so that one day I suppose I shall remember
this, and the flavour of love, and the music of ice
when I lift this glass. Also I wonder if
it will be pain or pleasure to remember these things
and whether, at last, I shall know which is which.

Remembering the Griffin

Sometimes, if I sat at the back of the bar,
as I often did, ignoring what happened on stage,
another mystery would reveal itself –
or half-reveal. Over to the left
the gauzy curtains of the private dance area
would be parted a little, and in the dim light,
the dim green–golden light, among glints of mirrors
and the small white classical sculpture on the mahogany shelves,
I'd catch a glimpse of one or two naked girls –
never a whole girl, and never knowing which one,
for always they seemed to have their backs to me –
giving dances, of course, to some customer.
There would be just the glimpse of their curves,
beautiful buttocks, perhaps a breast or a thigh,
or the sudden toss of a mane of hair, dusky or blonde,
falling down a pale back over which a bare arm might reach.
Always the unseen, the partly-seen, the loved, the lost,
and the hidden watcher. It was like memory in the making,
the secret, the illusion, the something beyond.
And in it was all the mystery of love,
as it seemed to me then: love at a distance,
love in a mist, love behind a curtain,
never wholly revealed, never quite hidden,
a mirage, a vision going beyond sight:
sold perhaps for money again and again,
but untouchable, precious beyond price.

The Cat in the Axe

Past the pink neon sign that says STRIPTEASE,
the bulky doorman and the mirrored doors,
a moiréd tabby slips, to curl at ease,
and yawn, and spread his pavement-blunted claws.

Last of the great cut-glass gin-palaces,
in plaster, brass and carved mahogany
the Old Axe hugs its smoke, its tranced-out guys,
its girls in nylon, lace and PVC

masked in a language whose fine shades distinguish
sex from allure, the offer from the tease –
telling sweet lies to customers in English,
keeping the truth Polish or Portuguese.

Under a table, safe beyond the range
of five-inch heels and polished city shoes,
serene, ignored, he stares across the strange
and predatory rites these creatures use.

Money, lipgloss, mascara do their work.
The dressed, half-naked and the nude perform,
reflected in those golden glints that lurk
still at the eye of the cosmetic storm.

Freed by his species from our best and worst,
he rests in tranquil, tigerish contemplation,
a necessary heart: watchful, immersed
and cool amid the human conflagration.

The Cave of the Nymphs

After Odyssey *XIII 96–122*

There is a cave that belongs to Phorcys, old man of the sea,
in the land of Ithaca, hidden between two pillars of rock
sheltered from the great waves raised by the turbulent winds
outside. In there, the well-built ships float without drifting
calm in their measured places, quietly riding the sea-swell
light as a girl's belly-chain on the smooth rise of her skin.

Here at the top of the cove there grows a thick-leafed olive,
and close to it opens a cave, lovely, twilit, shadowy,
sacred to those nymphs who are called the Naiades.
Down there are mixing-bowls for wine, two-handed amphorae,
all of stone; and there the honeybees build their palace.
And there are tall stone looms on which the tireless nymphs
weave their sea-purple web, a magical thing to see;
and there are streams of water that flow perpetually.
Two are the entrances: one up toward the north wind –
and by that mortals descend. But another faces the south –
divine, and not for humans. That is the path of immortals.

Here they drove into the shore, knowing the place already,
running the ship aground by fully half its length,
so hard the rowers impelled it. Leaving the sturdy ship's
benches for solid ground, they carried Odysseus first
out of the hollow hull to lay him down on the sand,
overpowered by sleep. Also they carried the treasures
which the noble Phaiacians had pressed on him to take
for his homeward journey, fulfilling the will of kind-hearted Athene.
And there they left him dreaming, close by the olive-tree's trunk.

Private Dance

I

What are we doing here? Haven't we got
jobs or homes to go to? Yes indeed,
that's why we're here. This is the place we're not
supposed to be, the place for when we need
all the things someone said we shouldn't have.
As one melts to one-thirty, then to two,
the drinks and mirrors deepen, the girls behave
like perfect ladies, and we come to know
that we're in sanctuary this afternoon,
a rich dim island rounded with the flow
of music, taste, desire in circulation.
Somewhere else, far away, work has to be done
(tell us about it). What we want right now
is darkness, cigarette smoke, pink neon.

II

The music's not just visceral, it's savage.
The bass hits you with an edge of hysteria
that says, look, nothing's ordinary here:
expect to be ripped, turned inside out, subjected to damage
and yes, fucked over by the power of what
you're about to see. Then a girl strides into the circle
of spotlights, gives you one look and turns on her heel
to spread her legs, pull up her skirt, slam her hot
palms onto the mirror and show you her arse,
a lit peach, cleft by the black line of the thong
which you know she'll start to roll down any minute,
though first she's going to discard that tight white dress –
and you also know this is exactly where you belong,
this is what you came for, the meaning of life so far, the unmistakable hit.

III
Christina

Christina is a minimalist. It's all
done with looks. She hardly seems to move.
Her infinite slowness peeling garments off
torments the punters. Her ferocious scowl
frightens and fascinates us. She's so cool,
so blonde, her breasts so wholly aureole
and mango-like and soft and they so loll
out from her corset! She leans back on the pole,
slides her white lace skirt up (she doesn't wear
knickers) and strokes that haze of golden hair –
dreamy, as if she doesn't know we're there –
then suddenly she'll catch your eye and smile.
It's weird. It's memorable. It's what you call *style*.

IV
Shannon

Shannon's the secretary from heaven – or hell,
whichever you prefer. Dark, piled-up hair,
pinstripe jacket with padded shoulders, a pair
of huge-rimmed spectacles – you can't quite tell
if it's a challenge or an invitation
that meets you in those too-observant eyes,
though the black stocking-tops and creamy thighs
suggest she might take more than just dictation.
The real delight is her manipulation
of audience: how she'll intimidate, and flirt,
and let the front-row guys look up her skirt,
but never quite conform to expectation –
keeping the jacket on, sulky, alert,
catlike, unsettled; all her own creation.

V
Misty

Misty is (as you might guess from the name)
Canadian. She radiates that entrancing
Vancouver-innocent look. Which, when she's dancing
naked but for a pair of black platform
boots on a glowing stage in a dark room
full of strangers, packs quite a charge. Enhancing
the weirdness of it is her way of balancing
slender, leggy, on the pole in some
of the trickier yoga positions. The appeal
is specialised and I don't go for it,
but watch her cruise the bar at a leisurely stroll:
White blouse, thin legs, tiny green tartan skirt:
though none of it actually screams schoolgirl,
I can't help feeling that's what she's about.

VI
Nicole

Nicole's a fire that carries its own dark
sphered round it. Night sky round star, shadow round flame.
Her cloud of black hair, her vermilion lipstick
focus a room's attention with the same
harsh, spare language as the red chiffon
scrap that passes for her dress, her eyes
selecting each of us in turn for seduction,
seeing into us, then denying it: the typical Gemini's
lightspeed supernova attack. I try to observe
calmly, but each time I'm caught in the beautiful lie
told by her smile's pristine, childish curve,
which says *I just can't help it, I'm hopelessly
in love with you.* How can she have the nerve?

VII
Carina

Vertical light. The way she steps on stage –
tall, pink-and-honey-tanned Brazilian blonde
with a piercing sapphire gaze – puts her in charge.
Shoulders, professional spin, make a clear demand
for your total attention. Watching herself in the mirrors
she slides the dress off, scoops each breast up, licking
the nipples dreamily, then returns your gaze
to check out how you like your chance of looking,
unhindered, into her private/public world.
Narcissism's her way to your heart. Bending
right over now she strokes herself with a finger,
arches up, shakes the music out of her gold
hair and turns away from us, to end standing,
defiant, up against her reflection, a moment longer.

VIII
Nicole and Carina

Girl on girl: plenty, profusion, excess –
a river of jewels, a mountain of flowers; a sweet
hot chocolate-sprinkled *latte*, Nicole says
mischievously, slipping one of her feet
between Carina's, lifting the blonde girl's thigh
against her own, coffee flooded with cream:
two beauties twined together, each with an eye
for how I'm watching them watch me watch them.
Carina undulates to bring her breast
against Nicole's, laughing at my delight
in seeing two lovely hemispheres compressed,
yielding and firm, the dark against the light.
Renaissance *chic*: hearts, eyes and worlds conspire
in pure triangulations of desire.

IX
After Baudelaire, 'Les Bijoux'

Knowing just what I like, she keeps her jewels on
when she strips, so stone and metal gleam
and clash: she's slave and conqueror in one,
light and sound melting in a single dream.
She crouches, but won't let herself be loved,
fixing her gaze on mine, a tigress tamed
by lust and music, a body restless, moved
from pose to pose, erotic, unashamed,
that sleepy smile enhanced by her vermilion
lipgloss; the oiled mahogany of her thighs,
her arms, her arse; an angel of destruction
with childlike candour radiant in her eyes –
until the song ends, and the red spotlights flood
her dark skin with a pulse that glows like blood.

X
After Cecília Meireles, 'Segundo Motivo da Rosa'

I go on praising you, but you don't listen,
lost in the tides of music where your body
surfs, turning its curves, blondes, its shell-pinks –
spoilt goddess-daughter of that uttering sea.
Let me imprison you in the wall of mirror
beyond spotlight or bar, hold in memory
your absent look, your perfect emptiness,
the glass you fill for every wasp and bee
just as for your lover, O deaf and silent
and blind and beautiful and endless rose,
transmuting to time, perfume, poetry
everything of yourself, a star glittering
somewhere outside my dream, not even knowing
your own beauty because you never listen…

XI

Black jacket, charcoal shirt, silk handkerchief,
a splash of Givenchy *pour homme* today
(chilled summer fragrance, throwing into relief
the girls' hot favourite, Jean-Paul Gaultier) –
dandy of words, I haunt here like some thief
of love and looks from Hoffmann or Genet.
What sparks the vision isn't only sex:
trash-glitter bras, lip gloss and platform shoes,
red satin bows, long-arched backs and bare necks
mirrored in amber light chime with the blues
of a Picasso circus, Toulouse-Lautrec's
music-hall dancers, or Manet's barmaid, whose
tired, quizzical gaze seduces and endures –
I'm here for art, that's my excuse. What's yours?

XII

No excuse needed. You're in love with all this –
art, nakedness, sex, beauty, the hidden:
this whole place gives a natural expression
to something in you. You've been at home here always.
It's like somewhere you've visited in dreams
and now found your way back to. Talk to the girls
and they're your kindred spirits. Something spills
glistening from angled bodies, from music, it seems
a world confined and rich as the heart of an opal,
a mine loaded with occult ore. The erotic –
recognised, invoked, adored, enjoyed –
is what you taste and smell here. It's a temple
to the secret, the other, the under, the exotic.
You're clothed but you're naked. You're glad there's no place to hide.

XIII

What the hell am I doing here? It's a question
that often puzzles me too, one I like to reflect on
whilst queuing, say, at the bar, or in between
the acts, once I've dug out a pound coin
ready to drop in the pint glass of the tall girl
who's working her way through the crush and will be here shortly
in her seven-inch stilettos and red bikini,
treating each customer to that wide-eyed schoolmarm smile.
You might talk about my relationship with my mother
or my anima or mirrors or even my addiction to poetry,
but just for the moment if you don't mind I'd prefer you
not to talk at all, because as you can see
one possible answer is going on stage right now,
and the question is where we should stand for the best view.

XIV

The pole is *axis mundi*. Some medieval
angel who steered the world might look like this,
grasping the cosmos by its silver spindle,
turning the spheres to spin out time and space.
But she's the image of some stranger goddess
also, reflected in the mirrored wall:
the shaman's bride, the naked pythoness,
the flamelapped mistress of increase and fall.
And Angie's eyes are rapt, her gaze secluded
in private realms I can't interrogate –
though I can read her body-language, loaded
with knowledge from the world-tree's deepest root:
all but the dance itself to be discarded,
and trampled, like her garments, underfoot.

XV

Left of the stage, two men in suits confer.
A finger taps a waistcoat: 'Don't for*get* – '
The deal is struck, the ball-park figures set.
The dancer's close; they don't acknowledge her.
They've watched the NASDAQ and the FTSE sink,
rally, then sink again. They've kept their nerve,
now daren't look parched for what they both deserve,
a naked woman and another drink.
The dancer pouts and shakes a golden mane:
the plump chap sidles off towards the bar.
She spins slow magic, peeling off her bra.
The thin chap glances, looks away again –
pooled in red light, flanking the stage, alone,
punching the digits on his mobile phone.

XVI

Carina can't make some of these guys out.
'It's like I'm giving them a historical tour!
I shake my tits at them, they look like *that* –'
She mimics a glum mask. 'Okay, what more
should I be doing to keep them interested?
I take my knickers off, they sit like *this* –'
A slumped, glazed look. 'They're so inhibited!
It's the applause, the *eye*-contact I miss.
Back home in Rio, there's this club I know –
we go to watch men strip. My God, the noise!
The girls shout, scream, they claw the dancers – Oh,
we're so fired up we almost *kill* those boys!'
She smiles dreamily, living it all again:
'*Meu Deus*, the women are so much worse than the men!'

XVII
Striptease

Wish-fulfilment. Fantasy in fact.
Western artistic tradition: the female nude.
Diana, huntress, glimpsed dangerous in the wood.
Slutty mistress you longed for. Secret pact
that you'll both be shameless, frivolous, discard the cooked
for the rawer the better, the rules for the carnival. Bud
opening into flower. Venus readying for your bed.
Rough rock cut back to gem. Luscious gift unpacked.
Journey from complex to simple. Primal scene.
Complicity. Innocence. Eye-contact. Addictive image.
Transgression. Decoding. Sweet painful suspense. Wet dream.
Apotheosis of clothing. Theatre of seduction.
Offering of self. Poem revealed by turning page.
Vulnerability as power. Truth unveiled by time.

XVIII

You take it all as utterly sincere:
unthinkable that I should simply mime
passions and looks that bring us both so near
to sharing, for an instant out of time,
unspoken knowledge of what love might mean –
the body's language and the heart's delight,
the hidden fires that rage under what's seen,
the gulfs and echoes where we go at night.
It's what I do. So if you like it, take it.
Before and after all the hurt explaining,
I have to feel it so that I can fake it –
no point in my self-doubt or your complaining.
At least there's enterprise in walking naked;
the truest poetry is the most feigning.

XIX
Street Clothes

Wasn't it Yeats who warned against confusing
the poet with 'the bundle of incoherence
who sits at breakfast'? Equally amusing
and startling, the sameness and the difference
between this average girl with bags of shopping
and woolly coat, hurrying in off the street
trailing her small wheeled case, just briefly stopping
to check what time she's on, or maybe greet
a friend already working – and the blaze
of sex and glitter who strolls onstage to strip
half an hour later. In our dreams, our days,
love, art, or anger, we've all made that trip,
on cue or off: oracular, naked, numinous –
powered by those forces we once thought weren't in us.

XX
Hotel California

The echoes are far too poignant. That '70s chime –
American twelve-string Gothic falling through space –
painted deserts, spilt sunsets, South-Western sublime.
Gabrielle untwines from the shadows, turning her face
from blazing mirror to bar: her sullen-lipped grace,
señorita good looks, long bare legs, those ruffled skirts
lifted and shaken, a glance so inviting it hurts –
tequila with lemon and salt, Corona with lime.
Some dance to remember, she sings, *some dance to forget*,
the red light dusting her body like memory,
and we know what's coming: *You can check out any time
you like, but you can never leave.* And her look hits the target:
eye-to-eye contact, she throws the last phrases at me –
she knows what music the old men like to see.

XXI

Why do I remember Sir Thomas Wyatt
so often in this place, in these poems?
Is it just his domestication of the sonnet?
Or the thought of one quietly observing women in rooms
goldleafed with so much archaic ritual,
so much hidden power loading the male and the female,
that the loosening of a dress or echo of a footfall
are momentous events impinging on the spiritual?
When I watch how Diana slides onto a bar stool
near the notice warning that anyone touching a dancer
will be asked to leave (i.e. thrown out by the bouncer)
I shiver as if Dante's *Amor* passed by, and recall
'*Noli me tangere, for Caesar's I am,*
And wild for to touch, though I seme tame...'

XXII

Why are there so many mirrors? Nobody asks,
nobody seems to notice. But I do.
It can't be merely to give us a better view
of some girl on stage who happens to turn her back
at the wrong moment. It isn't just so we can look
at ourselves, those strangers, immersed and transformed by this too
intense, sticky, theatrical sensory fondue
of colours, fantasies, perfumes. Surely it's so
that a wall isn't merely a wall nor a door a door
but each space flows into others, further and more
insubstantial, prolific rooms that model our dreams,
the sweet labyrinthine recessions of desire,
darkly glittering realms in their carved gold frames,
half-seen faces melting in shadow and fire.

XXIII

Evening outside. Here in this curtained room
a time measured by fantasy persists.
Sliding her dress off, smiling in the gloom,
the girl leans forward, offering her breasts
for my approval, making eye-contact
as if we should acknowledge what we do
before the next adroitly angled fact
of flawless flesh is opened to my view.
Here art is what we fight with, love, and sell:
both have our secret reasons, our mundane
motives besides. Chasing the beautiful
each through the language of a different pain,
we reach the music's end, the time to pay:
one kiss, one smile, one nothing more to say.

IV

… ungerührt flattere ich von den Lippen der Helena auf die Wunde des Adonis, ich liebe meinen Tod die Flamme über alles.

… unmoved, I flutter from Helen's lips to Adonis' wound. I love my death, the flame, more than anything.

Hugo von Hoffmansthal

Scattering the Ashes

At last the rain cleared and we found a barley-field
where the crop was knee-high, and in our town shoes
paced the lumpy furrows along the edge
until our trousers were soaked. My brother held it out,
open, and I pushed my hand in. It was like
dark corn, or oatmeal, or both, the fine dust
surprisingly heavy as it sighed through the green
blades and hit the earth. And like the sower
in that nursery picture ('To bed with the lamb,
and up with the laverock') we strode on, flinging it
broadcast, left and right, out over the field.
And there was no doubt that things were all in their places,
the tumbled clouds moving back, light in the wheel-ruts
and puddles of the lane as we walked to the car;
and yes, there were larks scribbling their songs on the sky
as the air warmed up. We noticed small steps
by a pool in the stream where a boy might have played
and people fetched water once, and wild watercress
that streamed like green hair inside the ribbed gloss of the current.
And then I was swinging the wheel as we found our way
round the lane corners in a maze of tall hedges
patched with wild roses, under steep slopes of larch
and sycamore, glimpsing the red sandstone of castles
hidden high in the woods. And the grit under our nails
was the midpoint of a spectrum that ran from the pattern in our cells
to the memories of two children, and it was all right.

Amanita Muscaria

Come with me, sweetheart: shall we make the trip?
Late one wet summer, on a narrow path
through a pine-forest. Can you still make it out –
the glazed vermilion cap with papery white
blisters; and the shadows beyond?

Fly agaric. The largest ever seen,
surely, its varnished scarlet canopy
fleshy and dented, white umbrella-gills
like turbine-blades at one edge where it tilts
a skewed, hallucinatory table-top

for us to feast our eyes on. Thirty years,
or nearly, it has ripened in the past,
intricate alkaloids neurotransmitted
to ride the gentle slopes of memory,
turning the air of that day to a brew

visionary as fermented mare's milk –
the smell of tamped pine-needles, the shush
of conifers around us whispering, whispering.
We were young and together, travelling
for the first time. The smallness of your hand

is new this moment, your green army-surplus
wool-collared jacket furry to my touch.
Those were the days of dope and LSD.
But we have drunk a stranger drug called time –
are bleached, reshaped, wizened to simulacra

we would have shied from in half-recognition
had we turned round to see the pair that now
look through their younger eyes. 'And so you think
you're changed, do you?' the caterpillar asked.
'I'm afraid I am, sir,' Alice replied.

'Changed and not changed,' I think I might have answered;
and today cannot, while it lasts, resist
tasting a fragment of that notched fruit-body.
'Which side?' Alice cried, 'O which side?' –
finding no way to judge of right or left

where one edge would enhance, and one diminish.
We have no choice, we are already beyond it,
can only reach back to the hither side,
recall what we can, and taste what we recall.
Quick, lover, bite now. Tell me, how does it taste?

It's our own fragile flesh, and its flavour is love.

The Blue Room

The blue room is full of the rowan tree:
what is outside the window fills the space
so that lamp, desk and even the tropical fish
are lit and shadowed by those scarlet boughs,

those scarlet-clustered twigs that once were cream
of lace, the winy flowers powdering grass-
green filetoothed slips of leaf so plaited in
the sky could hardly glint between their lashes.

That was in spring, and now the autumn calls
out waxred berries as the brownedged leaves
grow tired and tone their dusky greens to olive.
But the scorched edges never end the story,

and by October gold-and-orange flames
with delicate serrated tongues will hang
from every twig, while tousled flocks of starlings
havoc the bunches down in red profusion.

I can remember the bare twigs of winter,
budded already: but the tree is dreaming –
erect on fountains of the northern sap
that siphons slowly in its bundled veins –

of rockfalls and the feather-creeping lichen,
of women knotted as a stormbent treetrunk,
of the king's son and how he came to harbour
safe in a ship whose keel was cut from rowan-wood,

of how the witch-queen couldn't move to harm him.
And my son sleeps the better though the window
is open to the sky of blue September,
sleeps soundly, and the cat sleeps curled beside him

as if the room were upheld by the branches,
as if his dream grew there outside the window,
as if the house could offer no protection
and needed none, being full of the rowan tree.

From the Hexagon: Yndooroopilly, NSW

For Barbara Blackman

An old wood rocking-chair bleached by the sun,
spread with a crocheted quilt whose colours run
to faded pastel in the evening light –
good seat to rest in, and enjoy the flight
of this wood hut that floats over the green
gulf of the forest; nothing in between
its plain plank balcony and the sandstone bluff
that juts, a craggy island, from the rough
ocean of trees spread out to the world's edge.
The chair and I are safe upon a ledge
of domesticity, with the old broom,
firewood and battered kettle, and the room
behind us with its stove and bed. But sleep
isn't for now, although blue shadows creep
out of the gorge, dull the white-trunked gum trees
and carry up a music on the breeze –
a birdcall like an echoing scarlet kiss,
a flute-trill, or another like the gliss-
ando of glass beads rolling in your palm.
All is made possible by the strong charm,
the magic circle, of the house above,
built out of hospitality and love,
mud-brick, tree-trunks and corrugated tin:
a place where magic and the gods look in
to light the lamps, cut bread or taste the wine;
where friendship, art, hard work and dreams combine.
A house that calls out to the distant peaks
and to our hearts, in the same moment, speaks
of secret hopes and present comforts. So,
while wind and birdsong harmonise below
and the cold shadows climb up from the valley,
I praise the luck that shaped Yndooroopilly
and gathered us into its glowing heart,
before dreams, roads, lives carry us apart.

Toward Michaelmas

Now that summer is dying, and September
already eating the wet flower heads,
a medieval exuberance riots at the edge of the allotments,
a feast of colour already rolling back
with the lowering sun towards a dark age.

Brambles hurl their fanged and barbed curlicues
over a brick wall's broken corner,
and the marginal illumination of nasturtiums,
trumpeting and green-plated, vermilion, orange, mustard,
striped like a jester's coat and feathered bloodcrimson
with the fine paintbrush of light, shivers with air and praise.

Blue alkathene tube swirls a swash-
capital beside a shed, and bluer alkanet
dots the detritus and dead grass by the fence.
Strings of convolvulus embroider the empty parrot-cage
and a man in broad corduroys is bending,
far off, to scrutinise, deep in the soil,
glints of not much; whose very meagreness
satisfies him, no doubt, that for next year something is left.

Total Eclipse

Summer is over: the sunflowers droop in their jug,
blotched leaves guttering over the rim,
and the huge faces, dusky chocolate velvet,
bloom an unearthly dark. Clocks without hands

whose time has wandered off with the blue skies
into a muggy haze of thunder-clouds
where almost-rain lies sweaty on the skin
and the children have homework at weekends. Now we must eat

what's left of the year, picking the summer's carcass
for the last few raspberries, the odd chapter
of the book we meant to finish on holiday,

and the sunflowers nod their agreement, heavy-headed
and ready for sleep, the black discs programmed
with small dreams of other seasons their genes will live.

The Peacock

Michaelmas daisy, latest flower
to tempt the old sun and new frost,
glows by the wood a final hour
before the heat of day is lost

and one drab peacock butterfly
drifts through the sharp October light,
to quiver notched and faded wings
leafbrown against the mauveish white.

Its summer namesake was a bird,
emblem of watchfulness and pride;
but time has left the name absurd –
worn, perforated, shadow-eyed,

the brittle traveller takes her rest,
nuzzles the flowers to find her food,
and has some hours to live at best;
night, cold and death are in the wood.

Stubborn survivor, in a cloak
like a torn carpet stained with dust
and wine and dew and battle-smoke,
the peacock drags her gold and rust

and clambers on the anther-tips:
her happiness gleams rich and dull.
I share the pungent taste she sips;
the flowers of death and life are full.

After Christmas

How is it they come out from the curtains,
in the days after Christmas, the old ghosts –
when the shortest days are already gone, and the true
frosts and snows of January not begun?

The enormous labour of preparing Christmas
has given birth to something quite unexpected,
and the old year, booted and bearded, has delivered
his last load of mischief to lay on our hearthstones.

Now the grey sky shines like a plate of marble;
there are gale warnings and a few leaves in the air
tossed like souls between the worlds, wondering
where to settle, our garden or another's.

In the exposed depth of the stripped woods
under the holly and the drifted beech leaves,
and in the rust-spots of the unstarted cars,
the time and the space are brewing a new year.

You can see the past months, like an enormous arch
of costumed figures from Shakespeare or the Tarot
with garlands of flowers, knives, bundles of fruit
and more puzzling emblems in their capable hands,

about to settle into the fresco of memory
but not yet sunk to sleep. And there's a space
that goes like a wedge down to the earth's centre
allowing us all to come and go as we choose,

the quick and the dead. Some shop to forget it.
Others plunge in to drink that rare element, tasting
neither of the wild rose nor of ivy berries.
Out of their mouths the oracles are reborn.

Genius Loci

Sometimes, as death came nearer, it seemed to him
that he would not mind becoming a *genius loci*,
a small protecting deity, for this place
of folded green, silver-grey rock, May blossom,
with its glimpses of stars, roots and mud.
It could be, after all, only a brief diversion:
in a few, or a few thousand or a few million
years it would be burned or covered with ice
or the planet itself, or the universe, would disintegrate
or otherwise unbe. In the meantime
he could tend it, discourage destruction, gently induce
such continuities of use, language, pathway, skill
as could be sustained. Nourish the dew, mitigate the intrusion.
And when all was gone, as it would be, he could keep
at least some tracery, some crystalline seed,
some impression or whorled print of what it had been
as nucleus or hint or inspiration
for another corner of some other world,
mental or physical or in-between.
Nothing could be kept, of course: it was all evanescent
as the apricot-lace buttress of bunched and dissolving cloud
spilling now behind oakwood and white-rendered
barn above the red roadsign on the steep corner
where the fence was. None of it was either
physical or mental, it was all both and beyond both
but it was good and it was loved and there was something
founded within its lineaments that made clear
how in its slow, elusive being or non-being
it returned the love and was also a kind of guardian
to those who noticed. And sometimes it seemed the noticing
was more important than both, and would go on.

A Fortuitous Event

In memory of 'A.E. Ellis' (Derek Lindsay, 1920–2001); author of The Rack

Over the intercom, a woman's voice:
'He's dead. I'm sorry, it must be a shock.
I'll come down. No, he lived two doors away.
The house is up to let now. February,
in a road accident. He was knocked down.'
  So the thick glasses and the fear of blindness
prefigured something else; though it was reading
and pictures that concerned him most. The mind's
less fragile eye conjures the Arcimboldo
over his mantelpiece: face made of flowers,
a fugitive white butterfly capricious
above the head. He said that 'conservation'
had ruined it, but loved it nonetheless.
  Something more should have happened. His one novel –
about the TB sanatorium where
he'd spent the war – which Cyril Connolly
and V.S. Pritchett thought a masterpiece,
and Graham Greene had ranked 'with *Ulysses*,
Great Expectations and *Clarissa Harlowe*' –
sank without trace. I have my father's copy,
dedicated 'In grateful recollection
of a fortuitous event which led
to so many delightful meetings.' What
the event was, I've no idea.
                              Before,
fortuitously, I lost my address book
and with it his phone number (ex-directory,
of course) I used to visit once or twice
in a blue moon. He was always alone,
moving around inside his beautiful
and cold and slightly shabby house, among
German mechanical toys, French music-hall
posters (and on the stairs a zoëtrope –
or magic lantern? I'm not certain which)
as if the things weren't his, he'd wandered in,
and needed to apologise for being
caught.
        For a long time I thought he was gay,

85

though once, while he fetched glasses from the kitchen,
I browsed idly along a lower shelf
where two quite different private-press editions
of *L'Histoire d'O* (fine bindings, folio size)
surprised me; though I didn't take one out.

    Whatever secret life there may have been
is still more secret now. I wandered off
to stand, fortuitous, in the square garden
and stare up at the tall, constricted house,
dark between windows lit on either side.
Something more should have happened. Nothing did.
The rain grew heavier, other lamps came on.
At last some small decision made itself,
I left the square and headed for Chalk Farm;
the crowds, the traffic, and the Underground.

Untitled

In memory of R.S. Thomas

No, I don't fear it.
Long ago I was frightened,
it was like a tower of books
tottering,
about to fall and spill the knowledge of ages
and the work of my hands
crumpled, inkstained, into the puddles.
I tasted the fear and lived on it,
imagined the paper rotting
blown to the sides of the road,
becoming earth, and in the waters
the spring blossom reflected.
Permanence, that great stone monument
the poets carve for themselves,
lay in the corner of the workyard. Convolvulus drifted over it,
nettles put up a curtain,
the thrush sang and the half-cut inscription
stayed half cut. I preferred
the empty stone to the lettered.
Why should I panic
about time, which is not a line
but spreads around me, patched and collaged,
a palimpsest of memories mapped in all directions?
– Rather like this body, which ends at the edge of vision
and causes trouble or pleasure
accompanying me for a while;
or for that matter this mind,
now largely a repository
of the sort of things that were once in that pile of books
which tottered and may by now
have fallen.
Why should I care?
It will all have to go, and there is a secret joy
in knowing that: a joy with the same tone
as the open sky, the thrush's song
and the uncut stone. I would not say
I am eager for it. I would say, Let it come:
there is nothing here to hold on to.

To go beyond limits and boundaries
and, of course, beyond me
(the real nub of it all)
will be, simply, a relief.

A Dog at the Threshold

Coiled in a Celtic knot,
thin muzzle stretched on delicately crossed paws,
between the door and the singing fridge,
the dog sleeps at the threshold.

She could be sprawled on the flags
of some stone tower in a wilderness of reeds
between rough cattle-pasture and the sea,
while wind hammers the arrow-slits
and the fire flickers in a brown eye
momentarily opened;

or in the yard at Ty'n Llan,
where the farmer hauled her by the scruff of her neck
through a hole in the wire netting, over the ruck
of her yelping brothers and sisters,
orphaned since their mam
was killed getting under the feet of a cow.

Instead she rests on the lino,
half-trained to the garden and kitchen,
between leggy pup and lithe sheepdog,
and these are my dreams I wrap around her.
Black ruffled with white,
silver-horned with a crescent on the brow,
she is a focus for dreaming –
a lunar talisman
for this full-moon, autumnal equinox
illuminating an edge of the world that tilts
toward my fifty-first year.

It was my father died this summer.
Now with the dark of October
it's I who stand in the prow of that ship
with the wind in my face
and the three-headed dog of past, present, future
that bristles beside me, gapes
and grins with his riddle, the endless
interlocked triad of time.

Where did I think I was going?
to the islands of the blest,
to steer this house into harbour
beside golden orchards, where children
had the day's blue sky in their eyes
as well as the night-time stars,
and women would bring me honey
out of the wild bees' nest?

Or to trudge up the pebble-beach
alone, with the happy shipload
already fading in seamist,
to climb the steps of a tower
where a fire was lit and a meal waited,
near a book whose page was a door
into illumination?

We're always in the middle.
The dog grins and winks an eye,
the labyrinth of the page
extends in all directions.
The branches are black and the garden ragged
but still there is a garden:
oak, rowan, lilac, cherry
and grass shredded with gold –
powers of the natural world,
powers detected in the black of the ink
or the black-and-white check of the sheepdog's coat.

And there is love in its kinds,
the love of woman, of children,
and the love of animals
plaited into the design.
As winter brings worries about money
and occasional illness,
the route is unknown but the destination certain,
Scylla and Charybdis or the pillars of Hercules,
a rock and a hard place; and between them a dark gate,
the answer to the riddle.

Nor are the birds of poetry certain
to sing, though sometimes heard on the wind –
those birds with women's faces, 'whose song
wakes the dead and puts the living to sleep'.
And sometimes they drop a flower,
its dark heart the essence of its scarlet foldings,
knowledge petalled with sweetness.

Meanwhile there are things to be done.
You can't step over a sleeping dog without waking it,
so before I go out I offer this song:
honey-cake spiked with the poppy's bitter milk,
a sop for Cerberus.

Night

Slowly the night fans out
a peacock-tail of stars,
green into blue between
the eyes of Venus and Mars.

Slowly the sky comes clear,
speech with its disturbance
and all the rustling of paper
falling towards silence.

Time is for the day –
time is, time was, time's past.
But the night is timeless:
nothing first, nothing last,

preening the same black feather
out of her raven wing.
And her jewels are like the sea,
seething, endlessly soothing,

with a gold phosphorescence
poised on their rise and fall,
and a plunge deeper than galaxies
under the dark crystal.

Now everything is quiet,
not even a thought stirring,
the empty miles of the earth
begin to sing her a song:

a mythological symphony,
a music of all the colours
that can happen on earth.
And one of them is yours.

True or not true?
That belongs to the day,
speaking its daylight language.
Do not turn away,

but look into her eyes:
what she understands
is silence, darkness, love.
Give her your empty hands,

let your weapons go,
all the words that confuse you.
Enfold her, enter her.
She will not refuse you.